START A RIDING CENTER

Paul Abell

Kindle

*This book is dedicated to all Horse Lovers that ever wanted
to start a horseback riding center. You can do it! You
just have to know what is entailed and the cost.*

INTRODUCTION

I wrote this book to encourage people. I hope after reading it you will be knowledgeable enough to decide if you want to go through with starting your own center. I will give you all you need to know to startup a new riding center. With the background I am giving you, you should be able to hit the ground running and keep on going. Happy Trails!

CONTENTS

STARTING A NEW
Horseback Riding Center

CHAPTER 1. WANT TO START A HORSEBACK RIDING CENTER?

Do you want to start a riding center? Whether it is a Path, Intl. (**P**rofessional **A**ssociation of **T**herapeutic **H**orsemanship, International) riding center, your own version of one (Path member), or a riding center for the public, the steps below are common to ALL centers and are in place, (used), for a reason. The slant of this document is towards PATH compliant riding centers, but whether you want to start a certified PATH Intl. **P**rofessional Center or not would be the same for any riding center, just without Path guidelines being implemented.

What is your motivation?

Why do you want to do this? <u>No one</u> does this for the money! (Unless you are opening a horseback lesson/trail riding center for the public.). Your motivation can become extremely important down the road when difficulties arise. You can quickly arrive at the point where you throw up your hands and say, "God I can't do this by myself. I need help!" Horses will get sick or injured, volunteers will fail to show up without notice, instructors will quit and all of them will go on vacation or have family emergencies at one time or another. Things happen... If this is something you really want to do in your heart, then you will get through these little setbacks and you will succeed!

Can you afford it?

How much will it cost? This is almost impossible to figure with a rule of thumb, but lets say you already own and have in place everything you will need. Let's assume you already have:

A good convenient location
An appropriate number of horses
An instructor
Saddles, necessary tack
Available Parking

Additionally, you could figure you would **STILL** need the following:

Time - You have to be available 24/7 in the beginning, until you are established. This is not a part time career. How much is your time worth?

501(c)3 incorporation - $100-$900

Federal tax ID exemption - $50-$100

Certificate of Exemption - $300

Path membership - $50-up

Advertising to make the public aware - $10-$100-$100,000

Board of Directors - Your time and gas to assemble them for meeting.

Volunteers, getting and training - Volunteer manual printing costs, a place to train them, time to train them. Training instructors.

Riding center **Administration Procedures** - Collect money, schedule students, volunteers and run the business. Minimal cost depending on your procedures.

Develop and post a **web site** - $0-$300
This will serve you well as an advertisement, donation and information center, but is optional.

You are going to wind up spending around **$500-1000** to actually hit the ground running; open for business. Volunteers will <u>always be</u> your biggest challenge. This is why you need to instill in them the necessity of **<u>commitment</u>** at your volunteer training sessions! If you don't spend time training volunteers to all use the same techniques and procedures, you will wind up with chaos in the arena and around the barn. Consistency is paramount! That is why **Path** is such a good choice for an established organization to model and be a part of. If you use **Path** methods and practices, your students can leave when they have to move and go to another **Path** facility and keep on learning without a dropped step! No retraining required. This is your goal.

CHAPTER 2. BASIC PREPARATION

I have created and outlined a minimum of fifteen steps I think are necessary to start up a **Path compliant riding center**. Maybe fewer can be used if you are not concerned about using Path methods and techniques. When you model yourself after a particular organization, you are basically agreeing to everything they do, the way they do it, procedurally speaking.

There are more steps and considerations, but I would call these **basics**. You have to become incorporated to protect yourself from lawsuits and become eligible for a federal tax exemption. (charitable donations) You MUST check with a lawyer in your state to decide which corporation type will work for you and your center. You will normally <u>exist</u> on donations and volunteers and you will, if you are non-profit, need <u>plenty</u> of both. If you can't accomplish the above steps, (some can be quite challenging), you will struggle needlessly, but it <u>can be done</u>. Remember, where there is a will, there is a way. You have to be committed!

It's not as bad as it may sound. Some of the steps you probably have in place now and some steps, friends can help you with. Without help from a lawyer, it took us six months to get our **501(c)3** status. (Knowledge is power) It may not take you as long! You will benefit from a law clerk or secretary if you can find one to help you. It will be much cheaper!

I also strongly suggest you visit as many **Path Intl.** riding centers in your area (or local riding centers) as possible. Check out the **Path Intl.** website and look up existing centers. Find the closest to your proposed location and visit. Take pictures, ask questions, **plenty** of them. Ask them how they do this and that and why they do it that specific way. Ask, "How did **they** get started?" Take pictures of their facilities and how they are constructed, noting especially the size of the arena (dimensions, length and width), the mounting blocks and ramps used. (metal or wood) Notice what they are made of and ask if they have any construction plans available for them. (hard to find) Pictures can become invaluable later when you are back home and can't remember where you saw the ramp you liked and how it was made. I would recommend you take measurements of the ramps for later referral when you construct yours. If you have access to a handyman that can make it for you, pictures and measurements will help him greatly! Ours cost us about $400-$600 in wood alone. If it is going to be left outside it should be constructed from treated wood. Don't forget pictures of barn stalls. You will see many different styles and find one you really like. If you took a picture of it, you will save time when you try to duplicate it at your barn.

Although each center will be different and look different, all **Path** centers do things the same way for **Path** Intl. **consistency**. A student from our facility should be able to come to your facility and never skip a beat. We use consistent jargon, "**Walk On**", "**Whoa**", etc.

We groom and tack the same way, in the same order. This consistency makes the student feel confident and relaxed. All of the techniques and jargon are in the **Path Intl.** manual. If you are NOT going to be **Path** affiliated, just providing riding for the public, you can jump to step 5 and skip steps 7, 8, 14.

CHAPTER 3. INITIAL BASIC STEPS:

1. Do you have a **desire** to help children with special needs, or **anyone**, learn to ride horses?

2. Confirm step 1. This is serious business and you **will not succeed** if you are not 100% **committed**.

3. Create a mission statement. (**Very important**, this will be on almost every document you print.) Google, "mission statement" and read other centers mission statements, (on their web sites), to help you create your own.

4. Assemble a **Board-of-Directors**. (A minimum of: President, Secretary, Treasurer. These are necessary for a 501(c)3 corporation.)

Board of Directors
Board members need to be chosen for **specific** reasons. You need committed members that are influential in the community. This will help you in all you do, as the more people you know and have contact with, the more help and assistance you will get. Board members don't need to have any knowledge of horses to be a member, just a love for kids and helping people. Choose people with good, proven organizational skills. The more ties they have in the community, the more help they will be to you. You

need administrators, financiers, church leaders, politicians, etc. If you can find or get access to a grant writer, go for it. They will prove to be **invaluable** to you. Grant Writers are a God-Send to non-profits. Even someone that is willing to tackle Grant Writing would be a good choice. Grant Writing is tedious and you need to be familiar with the **techniques** used in grant writing to be successful. See Chapter 14 for more information on Board Members.

5. File for a **FEIN#** (Federal Employee Id Number; needed if you will ever pay an employee and to apply for a 501(c)3 status.) See **IRS** link publication:

http://www.irs.gov/pub/irs-pdf/p583.pdf

6. Get your states, **tax exempt** certificate. This allows your riding center to accept donations tax free. (varies from state to state) This allows you to purchase supplies for the center, tax free.

7. Decide which type of corporation you want to be. There are five distinct business structures available in the USA, including:

> Sole Proprietorship
> Partnership
> Limited Liability Company (LLC)
> S Corporation
> C Corporation

The three most popular structures are:

> Sole Proprietorship
> LLC, and C
> Corporation

8. Get your **501(c)3** non-profit incorporation status. ($100-$850) This will help keep volunteers, board mem-

bers and staff from being sued.

9. Join the **Path** Intl organization, (Center Accreditation - $500, $65 Individual membership), check with PATH for current prices. This is optional. If you wish to be a stand-alone organization or affiliated with another group, that's fine. It's your decision. They all have their own rules.

10. Locate a "place" to hold your lessons. You have to have space to ride, a barn for horses, some stalls, tack room, feed room and hay room, access to water and a phone if possible. (cell phones are great)

11. You can start on as little as 5 acres, possibly less, depending on the number of horses used.

12. One or more gentle, "Kid Broke", horses (this can be your **greatest challenge**) and the necessary tack.

13. *Time* to hold lessons during the week, weekends or both. You can become very busy, very quickly!

14. Initial set of volunteers, at least **three**. (Instructor, leader, side walker, if training children or special needs.) Don't forget to have some spare helmets for those that forget theirs. Some organizations will give your students a price break when they purchase a helmet if they say you sent them.

15. Hire a certified riding instructor. This will help you tremendously in the beginning and can even be you if you are working towards certification. It's not a deal breaker if you don't have one or have access to one, but they will certainly help you out in the long run. Borrow a riding instructor you trust to help you get started if you can't afford to hire a **Path** certified instructor. You can learn to become a **Path** certified instructor, (They have a course.) but it takes money and time.

See the appendix for a **checklist** to take with you when you visit other riding centers.

CHAPTER 4. ADMINISTRTION / VISITATION

You wouldn't think office administration would be too important when starting up a riding center, but you would be wrong. It is extremely important for your center to run smoothly and efficiently. OK, what does that entail?

Now, when we were just starting, we visited many riding centers and noticed that <u>office</u> <u>administration</u> <u>practices</u> were sort of left up to you! No one seems to cover this extremely necessary aspect of a riding center. I never got anything but vague answers when I would ask how they ran their center. See what you can learn from them.

Student fees varied from center to center and in different parts of the country. Ultimately, fees are left up to you and your board to decide how much to charge or even if to charge. Some centers use MS Excel, MS Word and Dropbox to do their record keeping and messaging, some QuickBooks, etc. Almost without exception, they all did it differently. Since we couldn't find anything already in place and readily available, we wrote our own software, called **Hana**. We also had to come up with our own forms and custom wording!

This can be an arduous, complicated process, since you don't

really know what you need or will need when you are just starting. (different states have different regulations) I have incorporated our custom forms into **Hana's** software so you can print out
any needed form with one click. You also have the option to customize them with MS Word (or an MS Word compatible program)
any way you want. Change them to match your local regulations
and preferences. This will save you an **enormous** amount of time!
Or, if you want, don't use them and create your own from scratch
as you need them. It's up to you.

You will need a release of liability form for your center volunteers and students, a volunteer log in sheet, barn worksheets and
many other things that come up as you go. After nine years now, I
think we have it all covered. We can even handle Field Trips from
local schools, military veterans, youth at risk and Horse and Me
programs.

Every center I have ever been to does administration differently,
even though they all have to accomplish the same things, use
the same processes, take care of horses, students, volunteers, etc.
Many use the same tools, just in different ways. As far as **Path** is
concerned, they don't seem to have any preferences in this particular area. I would advise you to invest in a 4 drawer locking
filing cabinet whether you ever use a computer or not. A used file
cabinet will do fine, as long as it works well. (drawers open/close
smoothly, locks)

CHAPTER 5. HANA (HELPING ACHIEVE NEEDED AGILITY)

Hana is the riding center software we use to accomplish all the tasks of our center. Using it we can do everything with one person, but three or more is really where you will be comfortable. It runs on a Windows PC, 7-10.

Below is a picture of the **Hana** main screen.

We sell **Hana** mostly on eBay and some other web sites. It comes on CD in a DVD box. A spiral bound manual is available for a small charge. You can edit and print all forms from within the program. No paper forms are supplied.

Check out the PATH web site.

www.pathintl.org

Search eBay for **Hana** under the category, software.

In our riding center, **Hana** takes care of managing some very important functions, like:

- ☐   • Volunteer scheduling, with email reminders.
- ☐   • Student lesson scheduling.
- ☐   • Saddle selection and assignment for each student.
- ☐   • Stirrup settings for each student.
- ☐   • Leader, sidewalker and Instructor assignment for each student.

- ☐   • Lesson Worksheet forms to post in the barn that outline all lessons for that day with info for each student, horse, instructor, leader, sidewalker, saddle, pads, stirrup settings and reins type and length. All this is printed on an easy to, read-at-a-glance, piece of 8 1/2 x 11 paper.

- ☐   • Student progress is noted after each lesson and stored for later reporting and review.

- ☐   • End of year reports tell how well a student has progressed based on parent surveys.

- ☐   • Complete horse care info is stored and recorded for historic purposes. Worming, farrier and vet appointments are tracked and forecast in available reports. Even pre-made Horse Placards with their pictures and vitals are available at a mouse click.

- ☐   • Forms are supplied for every conceivable purpose we could think of. All at the click of a mouse button, customized and ready to print. Forms such as:

Student Medical Releases
Student applications
Volunteer applications
Volunteer hour tracking
Volunteer Handbook

Scholarship application
Visitor releases
Volunteer time sheets
Barn emergency numbers and info
Lesson Plans
Daily Worksheets

These are not ALL the forms, but consist of the main collection. To have them already made up and ready for you to customize is a **very valuable** time saver. You will wind up creating every one of these forms over time by yourself if you don't have them or have access to them. **Hana** even comes with a small collection of signage forms we found useful. Things like **Whoa**, **Walk-On**, etc.

CHAPTER 6. IS IT WORTH IT?

Do we really make a difference in children's/volunteers lives?

YES! A resounding yes. Ask any volunteer/parent that is in a riding program if they have noticed a change in their student and they will all answer yes.

Our center gives each parent a survey form to fill out at the end of the year asking them to score how their child did in specific areas. The typical results follow:

Physical Improvement   - 63%   (this is outstanding)
Balance   - 32%
Muscle Strength   - 45%
Hand-Eye Coordination   - 25%
Dexterity   - 28%
Cognitive Improvements   - 30%
Emotional Improvements - 56%

These stats cover a wide range of disabilities, including Autism, Downs Syndrome, ADHD, Developmental Delay, Tourettes Syndrome, Spina Bifida, Cerebral Palsy and Vision Impaired. We don't get to see these dramatic results like the parents, who live with them 24x7, but by the end of the year you will see results!

The following is a statement from one of our volunteers, which has proven to be typical across our volunteer group. Everyone gets something out of volunteering!

"I was in psych class talking about drugs. We somehow got onto Autism and things like that. Someone said how they believe that people with Autism, no matter what kind or how severe, should be sterilized and locked away, which caused an uproar.

I stood up and stopped everyone and told my story of experiences at the riding center and a student, without using his name obviously, and how the riding center showed him he had a purpose. With that knowledge and purpose he began not only speaking, but taking better care of himself and how he ate got his weight down to be able to ride and started talking. I should have recorded the faces of people. The change in their faces was amazing.

After class, I was approached by a guy in the back. Guess who that was, the brother of one of our students. He was in awe of the way I stood up and stopped that and said he was glad I was one of the ones up there with you guys helping his sister. I almost cried. It was an awesome experience. I told my instructor that of everything I've ever done, from learning how to walk again, to watching my mother almost die before my eyes, volunteering up there was the hardest, but the absolute most rewarding. As soon as I get a schedule I will let you know!!"

We continue to get volunteer responses that encourage us with their amazement at what volunteering has done for them personally. Everybody wins!

CHAPTER 7. COSTS

So what are the basic costs you could get by with to start up? It all depends on how reasonable you want to be and/or how legal you want to be.

Actually, the horse can be the cheapest investment you make. You can get a horse very cheap, but you get what you pay for at horse auctions. **$300 - $1,000** should get you a good basic horse healthy enough for you to stay in business for 5 or more years. If possible, get a trail horse, preferably older, say 15-20 yrs old, that has been through it all and is not spooky or barn sour, but is willing to work. You can only determine this by riding them yourself. If you can find, "Kid Proof" horses, you will be starting out ahead-of-the-game. Some horse acquiring suggestions are; advertising in your local internet shopping network, Facebook, word-of-mouth, ask all your friends, Google are good starting points. You would be surprised at the number of people that no longer ride or the person that rode it has moved out and the horse just sits, are willing to get rid of their horse to the right person for next to nothing, sometimes free! You just have to look around, investigate.

A good horse will cost you about $1500 a year, in feed, hay, farrier and vet bills.

Tack - Saddles come in all sizes and styles and materials. MAKE SURE the saddle you get for your horse FITS! Saddle fit is **crucial** to your success. Lots of people that have gotten out of the business or no longer ride anymore will gladly give you a saddle or sell it to you for little or nothing. Mostly, they are glad to get rid of them once they are no longer being used. Garage sales, online local swap shops, etc are all good sources. Try to find an experienced horse person who can fit saddles. A bad fitting saddle will not always cause problems at first, but will cause some unusual horse behavior sometimes.

Invest in a **$5-$10 tack bucket** or tote. (Walmart, Dollar Store, etc.) You have to have something to carry around that will hold all your horse grooming tools. (brushes, combs, hoof picks, etc. Two of each tool, about **$50-$100**) You need two of each tool so the two sidewalkers can groom at the same time, one on each side. The tote keeps grooming tools in one place so they don't get lost and is handy. Also, a very important step, **LABEL** the tack bucket with the Horses Name and always use the same tack equipment for the same horse. Don't use one horses curry on another horse. Each horse should have their own tack equipment! This is hygienic and just good practice.

Invest in **horse signs** that outline state regulations in your state. Post them on your barn in plain sight. The cost is minimal, usually less than $10.00. You should have at least two.

Don't forget umbrella insurance for your riding center. This is a necessary expense and the sooner you get it the better off you will be. This can be an intimidating expense at first and you may not be able to startup with it. I urge you to get it as fast as you can, once you are open. Search the internet for providers.

CHAPTER 8. HOW MUCH SHOULD I CHARGE?

Boy, that is a good question! I would suggest you check with other stables and riding centers in your area and ask what the going rate is. If you charge more than them, you are probably not going to get as many students as you need.

You also have to decide if you are going to charge by the hour, day, week, month, session, etc. Come up with different fees for each option you offer. You will be surprised at what you find out when you start inquiring at other centers about what they charge. Ask them why they charge that amount. How did they come up with that? For non-profits, you have to decide what is fair and reasonable for your area. It will <u>never</u> be enough. You likely will have to offer scholarships, (another form), or point them to charitable organizations that support special needs children. Your state usually has one or two of these.

I suggest you start at **$25.00** per lesson. Either, non-profit or for-profit, that's a good starting point, though low for profit centers.

If you are only in it for the money, offer **boarding**. There is a lot of money to be made in boarding horses, with minimal work required. You really need to love animals and being around them or you will have to hire a barn manager. Boarding will always be self supporting, but once again, be careful and inquire in your area about the going rate and settle on a fair price. I have a boarding program that will get you up and running, called **BoardMaster**.

With it, you can potentially make **$1678** a year, ($150/month), boarding one horse in pasture, **$3242**, ($300/month), if in stalls. (you still have to provide feed, hay and water) This does NOT factor in vet or farrier visits or any special treatment or extras. Typically, the **owner** pays those bills. They can contract with YOU to do it, but you have to be careful and charge them up-front. Vet bills can get outrageous very fast! **BoardMaster** has a boarding calculator that lets you change all these parameters and see at-a-glance what a small change will make in the total for the year.

CHAPTER 9. LAND?

How much land do I need, where can I get it? Without a doubt, land will be your biggest expense unless you already have it, have access to it or can afford it. How much do you need?

It depends on whether you are going to provide riding services, horse training, horseback riding lessons, boarding, etc. You can start with as little as one horse, but you will keep it pretty busy. It's not good to work a horse for more than 3 hours at a time. They get tired and will burn out very fast and become unresponsive or get sick.

You can always add more horses, but you need the land to keep them on and barn facilities from time to time. It is suggested to allocate about two acres per horse for grazing purposes. So, I recommend 5 acres to start, with two or three horses.

You could consider leasing land and or facilities if necessary. Locating the right place is crucial to your success! Have a **Realtor** help you if necessary. You will need plenty of parking space for parents and visitors. Grass is OK, but can become a mud pit in wet weather and not very desirable. The more services you provide, the more parking you will need for things like horse shows, field trips, special events, birthday parties, open house, etc.

CHAPTER 10. FACILITIES

Your facilities are all important in your consideration of an existing place or farm. Keep in mind you will have to provide ample parking of some type and at least one **bathroom**. You will need an outdoor arena and if possible, an indoor arena! You will need a barn to house all your horses or at least as many as are going to be in a sessions worth of lessons for the day.

You need a feed room, tack room and a wash rack, plus cross ties or hitching posts, hay and bedding storage. You can combine the feed and tack room if space permits, but they are better separated. You want to have the horse you're going to use handy when the lesson starts. Also, you MUST plan on how to manage the manure that will be produced. On a daily average one horse can generate up to 50lb or more, depending on the size of the horse! This can add up quickly and get out of hand if not managed. A good pull behind manure spreader is great. A 25 cu ft. model will support up to 6 horses on a weekly basis. Some people just dump it in a convenient space and let it build. Try to sell it as fertilizer if possible. Picking up and dumping manure for 6 horses takes about 45 minutes, twice a day.

An office area is almost a necessity and very desirable if possible. If you are building a new barn or adding onto one, please consider adding a small 12x12 office area. Preferably with a window so you can bring in some light and have room for a window air conditioner/heat pump. Your office can be located anywhere, but it needs to be close to the barn. Your home is a good place if it is in close proximity. The more MULTIPURPOSE a barn is the more convenient it will be for all; don't forget the **bathroom**!

Mounting Blocks

Boy, these come in all sizes and shapes, even colors, but there is a pitiful selection of plans on the internet for building one. As you will discover in your field trips to other riding centers, there are more versions of mounting blocks than you can count! That's one reason you need to take pictures of them when you visit other centers. You will need outdoor and indoor mounting blocks. Check with your local building centers to see if they will donate the wood or at least give you a discount! If you are already a 501(c)3 when you purchase, you will get it tax free! Check with places like Lowes, Home Depot, Ace Hardware, Tractor Supply, etc. Tractor supply is probably already your best friend.

Mounting blocks can be as simple as a three step ladder or a three/two step resin plastic mounting block. (Jeffers, Big D's, Valley Vet and so on, all carry these in stock) There is a nice selection of portable metal ramp systems on the internet, but no wood versions. My recommendation is one with a ramp on one side and steps on the other. Each centers needs will vary. If you will email me and request mounting block plans I will send them to you. (PDF file.)

pgabell62@gmail.com

Lastly, some sort of signage with your Logo and farm name is very helpful to new people or passers by who never knew you existed until they saw it.

CHAPTER 11. EMPLOYEES/ VOLUNTEERS

If you are Non-Profit you will need **Volunteers**. If you are "For-Profit" you will need **Employees** and Volunteers. Most established Non-Profits have one paid certified instructor.

Non-Profit Volunteers (Free)

Volunteers are a necessary and very helpful necessity. You CANNOT do without them for special needs riders. You need three volunteers per student typically, until they are able to ride well enough without them. Independent riding is always your goal.

You MUST advertise for volunteers. This is a lot easier these days, due to the internet. Facebook, etc.) Word of mouth is your best source and asking to speak to church congregations, social clubs, Kiwanis, political groups, womens groups, bible study groups, book clubs, etc. **Anybody** that will let you come and present your services to their people is what you want. Get the word out to as many people as possible. Radio stations and newspapers are very good about giving new businesses a free shot. Talk to the Chamber of Commerce and leave a few brochures and business cards for newbies. Universities are a great source of volunteers. They have many BS programs that require community service time for their students. Talk to the schools to see which departments would like to hear from you. Any special needs field, FFA, Ag department, Farm bureau, Land management, social services, occupational therapies, Fish and Game, etc. Once established, setup special awards for volunteers with the most hours or worked extra events, etc. Reward them in some way if you want to keep them coming back.

Very important!

<u>Always thank them for volunteering</u>

<u>every chance you get.</u>

Remember, all volunteers are short lived, they grow up, get jobs, get married, graduate, etc. You will always be looking to replace existing volunteers. You need to develop a volunteer training program and manual. (**Hana** has these built in.) This develops consistency and conforms to Path standards. It will make for a better, more efficient group of volunteers. Unity is key.

It takes about 30 minutes to groom and tack a horse to get them ready for the rider, depending on what you are going to be doing in the lesson. Always schedule your volunteers to arrive 30 minutes before the lesson starts so they can get the horse ready.

Also, very important is the **order** of lesson preparation. Volunteer should always get the grooming tack area ready before they get the Horse! We even made a sign and posted it next to the grooming areas that says, "Tack First, Horse last".

Employees ($$$)

Employees are necessary and have to be paid. You have to decide if they are going to be full time or hourly. Each type has it's own advantages. Many centers have both. If you have over a certain quantity of employees, set by your state, you will have to provide health insurance, take out taxes, social security, vacations, sick leave, maternity leave, etc. (Check into this.)

In other words, you will have to have a Payroll system of some sort. You can farm this out if desired. It takes a lot of record keeping, I can assure you. (**Hana** does NOT handle employees.) You will need to develop or purchase an employment application form or create your own. Keep in mind you will need to do background checks (Always a good idea.) and is a small, but added expense.

Keeping track of hours worked is another challenge for you that can be simple or complex. You will need to see how other centers do it to get a feel for what might be right for you. Somehow, you must track hours worked. You can use mechanical time clocks and cards or even some digital time clocks that just keep everything on disk and is off-loaded on demand. We use a time sheet that the volunteers fill out when they arrive and leave. This could be used for employees as well, but the opportunity for fudging and mistakes is a much greater potential risk. **Hana** has a Post Volunteer Hours module that allows you to enter hours worked in a clock format, computes hours and saves everything for you. It will work for employees too, but is not worded that way.

CHAPTER 12.
ADVERTISING

You can't advertise <u>too much</u> unless you are overbooked or swamped and have a waiting list. Then you can stop advertising, until things slow down. I know you can't afford to spend too much on advertising when you first start up, but there are some steps you will be well advised to take.

Design or have designed, a riding center **logo**. This can make or break you. The cost can be very minimal, but well worth it in the long run. Down the road your logo will be used over and over again in everything you publish or design. Medals, ribbons, trophies, plaques, t-shirts, hats, etc, will all carry it and proudly proclaim your business.

VistaPrint (One of many, but high quality.) on the internet is a great source to get quality business cards, signs, t-shirts, coffee mugs, pens, brochures, etc with your logo on it, quickly. You can start with just a few (small quantities) to cover yourself and a few volunteers or employees. (Don't forget your Board members.)

This is FREE advertising. As with anything, you need to check your local printing shops for competitive pricing. "Google" services online for other printing choices, you may find a really good deal. You will be surprised to see what some local shops are willing to do to support you, as YOU are local. We can get t-shirts with our logo for as little as $7 each.

Check with your local newspaper and radio stations about announcing your new business opening. If you are non-profit, check with your local United Way chapter to see if you can get added to their list for donations. Some local electric and gas companies have grant programs that can help you.

If you become a Path member, they usually provide you with a free ad saying you have just opened for business. There are many free publications that will give you free ad space when opening a new business.

CHAPTER 13. PUBLIC SPEAKING

I know this scares everybody *crazy*. I used to be the same way.

I can't do it! I'm not going to do it.

Let Mikey do it.

Well, someone has to do it or you will struggle needlessly. If you will just sit down with your thoughts and a pencil and paper, you can jot down a few key topics that outline your business and services. Almost all groups that invite you to speak or allow you to, will only give you 5-10 minutes. Some organizations will only give you a minute as they have so many groups to listen to in one meeting. A minute is NOT very long, so you need to learn to summarize what you do and the benefits, in a few, well thought out, sentences. If you love what you do you can easily talk for 5 minutes. Churches are a great place to start. Start with yours. It's good practice. They are almost always open to special needs anything and generally will be very supportive.

Here's a suggestion. After you have written out a presentation, use your microwave timer to time yourself or a watch. I like the microwave because it will go off after the preset time whether I am finished or not, letting me know how close I came to the prescribed time and how much I need to trim or add to. Practice until you get it right!

If you still can't do it and are petrified, see if maybe one of your Board members would do it for you. That's why they are there, most of them are good at it and will be glad to help and advise you.

CHAPTER 14.
BOARD MEMBERS

Board member? What are board members? I don't need no stinking board members! Well, maybe you won't, if you never incorporate. That is not an option if you are a non-profit. You have to have board members; three in fact. President/Executive Director, Secretary and Treasurer. At first, they can all be you, until you find someone to fill them and they come on board. They are considered volunteers and not paid.

Board members should be a mix of professional business and lay people, with a politician thrown in for good measure. Why the mix? Shouldn't they just all be friends and family members? There are some state regulations concerning family relationships on the same board, but you need to check your states rules first.

Best not to get the family involved with more than one position on the board. What you really need are creative people with connections and the more the better. You will find that different people will have completely different sets of friends and contacts that can help you immensely down the road. The more diverse the better.

If you can find someone with business experience, they can help big time. They have all the contacts you need. Politicians and lawyers, bankers, all know people and resources you would never have access to if they weren't on your board helping you. Grant writers are a blessing from God! Search them out and try to get one to help you. (Worth their weight in gold!)

Have <u>monthly</u> board meetings. Down the road you can adjust their frequency as needed. Tuesday and Thursday nights are traditionally the most available times for people with day jobs, but go with whatever the board settles on. Almost no one will be available for day meetings, so try for 6 or 7 pm and keep it as short as possible. Have board meetings to lay ground rules, create a budget and By-laws. Financial reports are critical for the board to see money/donations coming in and expenditures going out. Let board members know of every speaking opportunity that comes in and encourage them to go with you. Brainstorm with them to come up with other areas to share. Try your best to follow Roberts Rules-Of-Order in your meeting and things will go smoothly. You will be talking a lot about fund raising.

Appendix

Checklist

A checklist is provided to take with you to riding centers you visit. Fill it out and file it in your filing cabinet when you return home. This will help you in the days to come. Try to store any pictures you took also.

I would suggest you keep a telephone address book of all the riding centers you visit. These people are great contacts and can help you greatly. Use each opportunity to build up your list.

Riding Center Checklist

Center Name:_____ Date:_____

Address:_____ City:_____ State:____ Zip:_____

Executive Director/Contact:_____ Phone:_____

Opened:_____ Years in business:_____

Outdoor Arena

Arena Length:_____ Width:_____ Fencing Made of:_____

Filled with:_____ Electricity:____ Water:_____ Ramps:_____ Lift:_____

Constructed by:_____ Phone:_____

Indoor Arena

Arena Length:_____ Width:_____ Made of:_____ Fans:_____

Filled with:_____ Electricity:____ Water:_____ Bathroom:____

Stalls:_____ Office:_____ Constructed by:_____ Phone:_____

Lighting:_____ Windows:_____ Doors:_____ Ramps:_____ Electric

Lift:_____

Barn

Barn Length:_____ Width:_____ # Stalls:_____ Made of:_____

Center aisle:____ Concrete aisle:_____ Stall floor type:_____

Bathroom:_____ Office:_____ Wash rack:_____ Feed room:_____

Tack Room:_____ Warning/signage:_____ Barn rules:_____ Doors:_____

Bedding:_____ Bedding storage:_____ Manure storage:_____

Electricity:_____ Water:_____ Fans:_____ Heat:_____ Windows:_____

Mounting Blocks:_____ Type:_____ How many:_____

Students:_____ # Volunteers:_____ #Horses:____/Type:_____

Certified instructors:____ # Uncertified instructors:_____

#Paid Employees:_____Position:_____

Attendees:_____

(Who came with you?)

ABOUT THE AUTHOR

Paul Abell

I retired in 1999 with my wife and we and moved to Tennessee with three horses on an 11 acre farm. I have been here for 21 years now and have been teaching special needs individuals to ride horses for 11 years.

START A RIDING CENTER

This is the eBook. A print and Large Print version are available.

Starting A Riding Center